Disclaimer

The information contained in this book is for general informational purposes only. While every effort has been made to ensure the accuracy and completeness of the information provided, the author and publisher make no representations or warranties of any kind, express or implied, about the completeness, accuracy, reliability, suitability, or availability with respect to the information, products, services, or related graphics contained in this book for any purpose.

The author and publisher shall not be liable for any loss or damage, including but not limited to, indirect or consequential loss or damage, or any loss or damage whatsoever arising from loss of data or profits arising out of, or in connection with, the use of this book.

This book is not intended to be a substitute for professional advice or services. The reader should always seek the advice of a qualified professional in the relevant field. The author and publisher expressly disclaim any and all liability for any actions or decisions taken by readers based on the information provided in this book.

The inclusion of any links or references in this book does not necessarily imply a recommendation or endorsement by the author or publisher. The author and publisher are not responsible for the content of any external websites or resources that may be linked to or referenced in this book.

Finally, the views and opinions expressed in this book are those of the author and do not necessarily reflect the official policy or position of any organisation or entity.

Contents

Forward

I am pleased to introduce "Area Cleaning Managers Handbook" by Tommy Taylor. This book is a comprehensive resource for anyone interested in learning about the role of an area manager in the cleaning industry, and how to be successful in this challenging and rewarding profession.

As an experienced industry professional myself, I can attest to the importance of having knowledgeable and effective area managers overseeing cleaning operations. The cleaning industry is essential to maintaining healthy and safe environments in a wide range of settings, from offices and schools to healthcare facilities and manufacturing plants. Area managers play a critical role in ensuring that cleaning operations are efficient, effective, and meet the needs of clients and their facilities.

In this book, Tommy provides a thorough overview of the cleaning industry and the role of an area manager. He/she covers a wide range of topics, from building and managing effective cleaning teams to creating and implementing cleaning protocols, and everything in between.

What I appreciate most about this book is its practicality. Tommy has a wealth of experience in the cleaning industry and provides real-world examples and advice that area managers can apply to their own work. Whether you are new to the industry or have years of experience, you will find valuable insights and guidance in these pages.

I highly recommend "Area Cleaning Managers Handbook" to anyone interested in pursuing a career in the cleaning industry or looking to enhance their skills as an area manager. Tommy has done an excellent job of providing a comprehensive and accessible resource that will be a valuable addition to any cleaning professional's library.

Mark Pinnock
Zenith Partners

Introduction

Welcome to "Area Cleaning Managers Handbook". This book is designed to provide a comprehensive overview of the cleaning industry and the role of an area manager, as well as practical guidance on how to be successful in this demanding profession.

The cleaning industry plays a vital role in maintaining clean, healthy, and safe environments in a variety of settings, from office buildings and schools to healthcare facilities and manufacturing plants. The responsibility for ensuring that these facilities are clean and well-maintained falls on the shoulders of area managers, who oversee cleaning operations in specific geographic areas or facilities.

As an area manager, you will be responsible for building and managing a team of cleaning operatives, developing and implementing cleaning protocols, managing budgets, and ensuring that cleaning operations meet the needs of clients and their facilities. This is a challenging role that requires a diverse range of skills, including leadership, communication, problem-solving, and time management.

In this book, we will cover all aspects of area management in the cleaning industry. We'll start by exploring the cleaning industry itself, including its history, current state, and future trends. We'll then dive into the role of an area manager, including how to build and manage effective cleaning teams, create and implement cleaning protocols, manage budgets, and more.

Throughout the book, we will provide practical advice and real-world examples that you can apply to your own work as an area manager. We will also highlight common challenges that area managers face and provide strategies for overcoming them.

Whether you are new to the cleaning industry or have years of experience, this book will be a valuable resource for enhancing your skills as an area manager. I hope that you find this guide informative, practical, and inspiring, and that it helps you achieve success in this rewarding profession.

Area Cleaning Managers Handbook

1. An Area Manager's Role in the Cleaning Industry

In the cleaning industry, your role as an area manager is to oversee supervisors and cleaning operatives in a specific geographical area. This may involve overseeing multiple sites, supervisors, and cleaning personnel, as well as coordinating with clients and ensuring that cleaning standards are met.

You must have excellent communication and leadership skills to be successful in this role. You must be able to effectively motivate and manage your teams, as well as build strong client relationships.

You'll also need to be familiar with cleaning methods and equipment, as well as health and safety regulations. You must be able to create and implement cleaning protocols that meet both your clients' needs and the legal requirements of your industry.

Finally, an area manager in the cleaning industry is responsible for ensuring that cleaning operations run smoothly and that clients are satisfied with the level of service they receive.

2. Creating and Managing Efficient Cleaning Teams

Building and managing effective cleaning teams is one of the most important tasks of an area manager in the cleaning industry. To do this, you'll need to recruit, train, and motivate your team members.

Recruiting the right people for your team is critical. Look for candidates who are reliable, hardworking, and have a strong attention to detail. Once you've assembled your team, invest time in training them on cleaning practices and safety protocols.

To keep your team motivated and engaged, provide regular feedback and recognition for their efforts. Offer opportunities for professional development, such as training on new equipment or cleaning techniques. And make sure your team members have the necessary tools and resources to do their jobs effectively.

By building and managing an effective cleaning team, you'll be able to provide high-quality service to your clients while also maintaining a positive work environment for your team members.

3. Understanding Cleaning Chemicals and Equipment

As an area manager in the cleaning industry, you'll need to have a strong understanding of cleaning chemicals and equipment. This knowledge will enable you to make informed decisions about which products and tools to use for different cleaning tasks.

Cleaning chemicals can be hazardous if not used correctly, so it's important to be aware of the potential risks and how to minimise them. You'll need to understand how to properly dilute chemicals, as well as how to store and dispose of them safely.

When it comes to equipment, there are a wide range of options available depending on the cleaning task at hand. From vacuums and floor buffers to pressure washers and steam cleaners, there are different tools for different jobs. As an area manager, you'll need to understand which equipment is best suited for each task, and how to operate it safely and effectively.

By having a strong understanding of cleaning chemicals and equipment, you'll be able to make informed decisions that ensure the safety of your team members and the quality of the cleaning services you provide.

4. Creating and Implementing Cleaning Protocols

Creating and implementing cleaning protocols is a critical aspect of an area manager's role in the cleaning industry. These protocols outline the specific steps that need to be taken to clean different areas or surfaces and help ensure consistency and quality across all cleaning operations.

To create effective cleaning protocols, you'll need to assess the specific cleaning needs of each client and develop a plan that meets those needs. This could involve identifying high-traffic areas, determining which cleaning products to use, and developing a cleaning schedule.

Once you've developed your protocols, it's important to communicate them clearly to your cleaning teams. Provide training on the protocols and ensure that all team members understand the steps they need to take to complete each cleaning task.

Understanding the Cleaning Industry

The cleaning industry is a vast and diverse sector that encompasses a wide range of services, from residential cleaning to commercial and industrial cleaning. It is an industry that is essential to maintaining the cleanliness and hygiene of our living and working environments, and its importance has only become more apparent in light of the global pandemic.

One of the key features of the cleaning industry is its flexibility. Cleaning services can be provided on a one-time basis or as a recurring service and can range from general cleaning to specialised services such as deep cleaning or biohazard cleaning. This flexibility allows for the industry to adapt to the changing needs of its clients and to offer a diverse range of services.

In terms of employment, the cleaning industry is a significant employer in many countries around the world. It provides job opportunities for individuals with a range of skills and backgrounds, including cleaning operatives, supervisors, managers, and administrative staff. It is also an industry that offers opportunities for growth and advancement, with many individuals starting as cleaning operatives and working their way up to supervisory or management positions.

The cleaning industry is also regulated, with a range of health and safety regulations that must be adhered to. This is particularly important given the potential risks associated with cleaning, such as exposure to chemicals and biological hazards. As a result, companies operating in the cleaning industry must ensure that their staff are adequately trained and equipped to carry out their work safely.

The global pandemic has also brought a renewed focus on the importance of cleaning and hygiene, with businesses and individuals alike placing a greater emphasis on cleanliness and sanitation. This has led to an increase in demand for cleaning services and a renewed focus on innovation and technology to improve cleaning efficiency and effectiveness.

In conclusion, the cleaning industry is a vital sector that plays an important role in maintaining clean and hygienic living and working environments. It offers a diverse range of services and job opportunities and is regulated to ensure the safety of its employees and clients. The industry's importance has only become more apparent in the wake of the global pandemic, and it is likely to continue to be an essential industry for the foreseeable future.

The current state of the cleaning industry in the UK

The cleaning industry is a vital sector in the UK, employing over 1.5m people and generating an estimated £24 billion in revenue each year. The COVID-19 pandemic has had a significant impact on the industry, with increased demand for cleaning and hygiene services in both residential and commercial settings.

The pandemic has highlighted the importance of cleaning and hygiene, and businesses are now more focused on ensuring that their premises are clean and safe for employees and customers. This has led to an increase in demand for cleaning services, particularly for specialised services such as deep cleaning and disinfection.

In addition to the impact of the pandemic, the cleaning industry in the UK is also facing other challenges. One of the main challenges is the ongoing issue of low pay and poor working conditions for many cleaning operatives. This has led to calls for greater regulation and enforcement of employment rights in the industry.

Another challenge facing the industry is the need for innovation and technology to improve efficiency and effectiveness. There is a growing focus on using technology such as robotics and automation to carry out cleaning tasks, which can help to improve efficiency and reduce costs.

However, there is also a need for skilled workers who can operate and maintain these technologies.

The UK cleaning industry is regulated, with a range of health and safety regulations that must be adhered to. This includes regulations around the use of chemicals and personal protective equipment, as well as guidelines for safe working practices.

Overall, the cleaning industry in the UK is facing a range of challenges, but it is also a sector that is essential to maintaining clean and safe environments. There is a growing focus on the importance of cleaning and hygiene, and businesses are increasingly recognising the value of investing in quality cleaning services. With continued innovation and a focus on improving working conditions for cleaning operatives, the industry is likely to remain a significant sector in the UK economy.

Regulatory landscape in the UK for the cleaning industry

The cleaning industry in the UK is subject to a range of regulations and guidelines designed to ensure the health and safety of workers and the public. The regulatory landscape for the industry is complex, and it is important for cleaning companies and professionals to stay up to date with the latest requirements and guidelines.

One of the main regulatory bodies for the cleaning industry in the UK is the Health and Safety Executive (HSE). The HSE is responsible for enforcing health and safety laws and regulations in the workplace, including those that apply to cleaning. The HSE sets out guidelines and regulations around the use of chemicals and cleaning equipment, as well as guidelines for safe working practices.

In addition to the HSE, the cleaning industry is also subject to a range of other regulations and guidelines. For example, the Control of Substances Hazardous to Health (COSHH) regulations set out guidelines for the handling and use of hazardous substances in the workplace. The Personal Protective Equipment (PPE) regulations set out requirements for the use of PPE, such as gloves and masks, in order to protect workers from exposure to hazardous materials.

There are also a number of voluntary schemes and certifications that cleaning companies and professionals can choose to participate in. For example, the Cleaning Industry

Management Standard (CIMS) is a certification program that sets out standards for management and operations in the cleaning industry. The British Institute of Cleaning Science (BICSc) is another industry body that provides training and certification programs for cleaning professionals.

It is important for cleaning companies and professionals to stay up to date with the latest regulations and guidelines in the industry. Failure to comply with regulations can result in legal action and fines, as well as potential harm to workers and the public. Keeping up to date with best practices and certifications can also help to demonstrate a commitment to quality and professionalism in the industry.

Overall, the regulatory landscape for the cleaning industry in the UK is complex, but it is essential for ensuring the safety of workers and the public. By staying up to date with the latest guidelines and regulations, cleaning professionals can ensure that they are operating safely and responsibly, while also maintaining high standards of quality and professionalism in the industry.

There are also environmental regulations that apply to the cleaning industry in the UK. For example, the Waste Regulations 2011 set out requirements for the safe disposal of waste materials, including those generated by cleaning activities. The regulations aim to reduce the amount of waste produced by businesses and ensure that it is disposed of in an environmentally friendly manner.

In addition to health and safety regulations, there are also employment laws that apply to the cleaning industry. These include requirements around minimum wage, holiday entitlements, and working hours. Employers must ensure that they are meeting these standards and providing their workers with fair and safe working conditions.

Key HSE (Health and Safety Executive) regulations and guidelines that an area manager should be aware of:

1. Health and Safety at Work Act 1974: This is the primary legislation governing health and safety in the workplace in the UK. It sets out the general duties of employers and employees to ensure the health, safety, and welfare of all individuals at work.

2. Management of Health and Safety at Work Regulations 1999: These regulations provide a framework for managing health and safety in the workplace. They require employers to assess and manage risks, provide necessary training and information, and maintain health and safety records.

3. Control of Substances Hazardous to Health (COSHH) Regulations 2002: These regulations focus on the control of substances that are hazardous to health. Employers must assess the risks posed by hazardous substances, implement control measures, and provide training to employees on their safe handling and storage.

4. Workplace (Health, Safety and Welfare) Regulations 1992: These regulations cover a wide range of health and safety requirements related to the physical workplace. They include provisions on ventilation, lighting, cleanliness, temperature, and other factors that contribute to a safe and healthy working environment.

5. Manual Handling Operations Regulations 1992: These regulations aim to prevent injuries related to manual handling tasks. They require employers to assess and minimise the risks associated with manual handling activities, provide appropriate training, and implement control measures to reduce the risk of injury.

6. Provision and Use of Work Equipment Regulations 1998 (PUWER): These regulations focus on the safe use of work equipment. They require employers to ensure that work equipment is suitable for its intended use, properly maintained, and used by competent individuals who have received appropriate training.

7. Personal Protective Equipment at Work Regulations 1992 (PPE): These regulations require employers to provide suitable personal protective equipment (PPE) to employees when necessary and ensure that it is properly maintained and used. Employees must also receive training on the correct use and maintenance of PPE.

These are just a few examples of the regulations and guidelines that an area manager should be familiar with. It is important to note that the specific regulations applicable to a cleaning company may vary depending on the nature of the business and the tasks involved. Regular monitoring and staying up to date with HSE guidance and updates is crucial to ensure compliance with health and safety regulations.

Key employment laws, regulations, and guidelines that an area manager should be aware of:

1. Employment Rights Act 1996: This act provides the framework for the rights and obligations of both employers and employees in the UK. It covers a wide range of employment-related issues, including employment contracts, working hours, holidays, and protection against unfair dismissal.

2. Equality Act 2010: This legislation prohibits discrimination in the workplace based on protected characteristics such as age, disability, gender reassignment, marriage and civil partnership, pregnancy and maternity, race, religion or belief, sex, and sexual orientation. Area managers should ensure equal opportunities and fair treatment for all employees.

3. Health and Safety at Work Act 1974: While primarily a health and safety regulation, this act also imposes a duty on employers to ensure the health, safety, and welfare of their employees. Area managers should be familiar with their responsibilities in providing a safe working environment and implementing appropriate safety measures.

4. National Minimum Wage Act 1998: This act establishes the minimum wage rates that must be paid to workers in the UK. Area managers should ensure that employees are paid at least the minimum wage according to their age and employment status.

5. Working Time Regulations 1998: These regulations set limits on working hours, rest breaks, and annual leave entitlements for employees. Area managers must ensure that employees' working hours and rest periods comply with these regulations.

6. Data Protection Act 2018 and General Data Protection Regulation (GDPR): These regulations govern the collection, storage, and processing of personal data. Area managers should understand the requirements for handling employee data, including obtaining consent, ensuring data security, and respecting individuals' rights to access and control their personal information.

7. Trade Union and Labour Relations (Consolidation) Act 1992: This legislation outlines the rights and responsibilities of trade unions and provides protection against unfair treatment or dismissal due to union membership or trade union activities.

8. Maternity and Parental Leave Regulations: Area managers should be familiar with the regulations surrounding maternity, paternity, and parental leave, including entitlements, notification requirements, and the right to return to work after leave.

9. Immigration Act 2016: This act sets out the legal obligations for employers regarding the right to work checks and employing foreign workers. Area managers should understand the requirements for verifying employees' eligibility to work in the UK.

10. ACAS (Advisory, Conciliation, and Arbitration Service) Guidelines: ACAS provides guidance on various employment-related matters, including disciplinary and grievance procedures, flexible working, managing absence, and handling redundancies. Area managers can refer to ACAS guidelines for best practices in managing employment-related issues.

It's important for area managers to keep up to date with changes in employment laws, regulations, and guidelines to ensure compliance and fair treatment of employees. Consulting with legal professionals or HR experts can provide further guidance on specific employment-related matters.

Overall, the regulatory landscape in the UK cleaning industry is complex and varied. Area managers must be aware of the regulations that apply to their business and ensure that they are complying with them at all times to avoid potential legal issues and reputational damage.

key players that have a significant impact on the regulatory landscape. These include:

1. The Health and Safety Executive (HSE): The HSE is the main regulatory body responsible for enforcing health and safety regulations in the UK, including those that apply to the cleaning industry. They provide guidance on how to comply with regulations and can issue fines or legal action for non-compliance.
2. The Cleaning and Support Services Association (CSSA): The CSSA is a trade association that represents the interests of the cleaning and support services industry in the UK. They work closely with industry stakeholders to promote best practice and raise standards across the sector.
3. The British Cleaning Council (BCC): The BCC is an umbrella organisation that represents various industry bodies and associations in the UK cleaning industry. They provide a unified voice for the industry and work to promote and improve standards across all sectors.
4. The Department for Environment, Food and Rural Affairs (DEFRA): DEFRA is a UK government department responsible for environmental protection and food production. They set policies and regulations

around waste management and disposal, which can impact the cleaning industry.

5. The Department for Business, Energy and Industrial Strategy (BEIS): BEIS is a UK government department responsible for promoting business growth and improving the country's economic performance. They set policies and regulations around employment law and workplace health and safety, which can impact the cleaning industry.

Overall, these key players have a significant impact on the regulatory landscape in the UK cleaning industry. Area managers must be aware of the regulations and guidelines set out by these bodies and work to ensure that their business is complying with them at all times.

Career opportunities and paths available to area managers within the cleaning industry.

These include:

1. **Progression within the same company:** Area managers may have the opportunity to progress within the same company they are currently working for. This could involve moving up to a regional or national management role or taking on additional responsibilities within their current role.
2. **Moving to a larger company:** Area managers may choose to move to a larger company within the

cleaning industry. This could provide new challenges and opportunities for growth and development.

3. **Specialisation in a specific area:** Some area managers may choose to specialise in a specific area of the cleaning industry, such as healthcare cleaning or industrial cleaning. This could involve taking on additional training or qualifications to develop specific skills and knowledge.

4. **Starting their own business:** Some area managers may choose to start their own cleaning business, either as a franchise or an independent enterprise. This could provide greater autonomy and the opportunity to build your own team and client base.

In terms of career paths, area managers may progress to roles such as regional manager, national manager, or operations director. Alternatively, they may choose to move into a different area of the cleaning industry, such as sales or training. The specific career path will depend on the individual's skills, experience, and interests, as well as the opportunities available within the industry.

In terms of salary expectations, the average salary for an area manager in the UK cleaning industry is around £30,000 - £35,000 per year. However, this can vary depending on factors such as location, company size, and level of experience. More senior roles, such as regional or national manager, can command higher salaries.

The cleaning industry has seen significant growth over the past few years, and this trend is expected to continue in the future. There are several reasons why the industry is expected to expand, including an increase in demand for cleaning services due to the COVID-19 pandemic and a growing focus on sustainability and eco-friendliness.

One of the biggest trends in the cleaning industry is the use of technology. Advances in technology have led to the development of more efficient cleaning equipment and products, as well as the use of automation and robotics in cleaning processes. This has made cleaning more efficient, cost-effective, and environmentally friendly, and it is likely to continue to be a major trend in the future.

Another trend in the industry is the focus on sustainability and eco-friendliness. Consumers are becoming more environmentally conscious, and they are looking for cleaning products and services that are safe for the environment. As a result, companies are developing green cleaning products and services that are designed to be sustainable and eco-friendly. This trend is expected to continue in the future, as companies look for ways to reduce their environmental impact and meet consumer demand for environmentally friendly products and services.

The future of the cleaning industry looks bright. With a growing focus on technology, sustainability, and eco-friendliness, there are many opportunities for innovation and growth in the industry. As a result, individuals who are interested in pursuing a career in the cleaning industry can expect to find a wide range of opportunities and paths for career growth and advancement.

Being an area manager in a cleaning company involves a range of responsibilities and tasks. Here is a more detailed description of what an area manager can expect in their role:

Site Management: Area managers are responsible for managing a portfolio of sites and ensuring that each site is running efficiently and effectively. This involves supervising site supervisors, conducting site visits, and liaising with clients to ensure that their needs are met.

Site management typically involves overseeing and coordinating the day-to-day operations of a specific location or site. In the context of the cleaning industry, site managers are responsible for managing and coordinating the cleaning operations of a particular building or facility.

The role of a site manager typically includes a wide range of responsibilities, such as:

- ❑ Planning and organising cleaning schedules and tasks to ensure that the site is cleaned effectively and efficiently.
- ❑ Hiring, training, and supervising cleaning staff to ensure that they are properly trained and performing their duties to the required standard.

- Managing the budget for the site, including the purchase of cleaning equipment and supplies, and ensuring that all expenses are within budget.
- Developing and implementing cleaning policies and procedures to ensure that the site is cleaned in accordance with health and safety regulations and other relevant standards.
- Liaising with clients, building owners, and other stakeholders to ensure that their needs are being met and that the site is being cleaned to their satisfaction.
- Monitoring the performance of the cleaning staff and providing feedback and coaching as required to improve performance.
- Conducting regular inspections of the site to ensure that cleaning standards are being met and that any issues are identified and addressed.
- Ensuring that all cleaning staff are trained in health and safety procedures and that they are adhering to these procedures at all times.

Site management is a critical role in the cleaning industry, as it ensures that sites are cleaned effectively and efficiently, and that cleaning staff are properly trained and supervised. It requires strong organisational, communication, and leadership skills, as well as a deep understanding of cleaning procedures and health and safety regulations.

An area manager plays a crucial role in supporting site managers to ensure they are performing their job duties to the best of their ability. Here are some key areas where an area manager can offer support to site managers:

1. **Training and Development:** One of the primary responsibilities of an area manager is to ensure that site managers receive the necessary training and development they need to carry out their duties. This includes initial training when a new site manager is appointed, as well as ongoing training and development to help them improve their skills.
2. **Performance Management:** Area managers should work with site managers to set performance goals and expectations, and regularly review their performance to provide feedback and coaching. This helps site managers to stay on track and improve their performance over time.
3. **Resource Allocation:** Area managers should work with site managers to ensure that they have the necessary resources to perform their duties effectively. This may include staffing levels, equipment and supplies, and support from other teams within the company.
4. **Communication:** Area managers should maintain regular communication with site managers to keep

them informed about company policies, procedures, and any changes that may affect their work. They should also be available to answer questions and address any concerns that site managers may have.

5. Problem-Solving: Area managers should be available to help site managers solve problems that they encounter in their day-to-day work. This may involve providing guidance on company policies and procedures or helping to resolve disputes between site staff or with clients.

Staff Management

Staff management is one of the key responsibilities of an area manager in the cleaning industry. As the person responsible for overseeing the work of site managers and cleaning operatives, the area manager must ensure that all staff are trained, motivated, and performing their duties to the best of their abilities.

One of the key tasks of an area manager in staff management is to recruit and hire new staff as needed. This involves advertising job vacancies (newspapers, trade press, social media, word of mouth or referral schemes), reviewing CV's and applications, conducting interviews, and making hiring decisions. The area manager must also ensure that all new staff receive appropriate training to carry out their duties effectively.

Staff inductions play a vital role in familiarising new employees with the company's policies, procedures, and safety protocols, and it is the responsibility of the area manager to ensure that comprehensive and engaging inductions are conducted, providing a solid foundation for employees to thrive in their roles.

Another important aspect of staff management is performance monitoring and feedback. The area manager must regularly assess the performance of site managers and cleaning operatives and provide feedback on areas for improvement. This could include providing additional training, setting performance targets, and monitoring progress towards those targets.

The area manager is also responsible for maintaining good communication with staff, both individually and as a group. This involves holding regular meetings, providing feedback and recognition, and dealing with any concerns or grievances that may arise.

In addition to these responsibilities, the area manager must ensure that all staff are following appropriate health and safety procedures and are compliant with relevant regulations. This includes providing appropriate training and personal protective equipment where necessary and conducting regular safety checks to ensure compliance.

Overall, staff management is a crucial responsibility for an area manager in the cleaning industry. By recruiting and training the right staff, monitoring performance, providing feedback and support, and ensuring compliance with health and safety regulations, the area manager plays a key role in ensuring the success of the cleaning operation.

Client relations

One of the key responsibilities of an area manager is managing client relations. This involves developing and maintaining positive relationships with clients, understanding their needs and expectations, and ensuring that those needs are met through effective communication and problem-solving.

Effective client relations begin with clear communication from the outset of the business relationship. Area managers must ensure that they are aware of their clients' expectations and needs, as well as any potential issues or concerns they may have. This can be achieved through regular meetings, site visits, and frequent communication via phone or email.

In addition to effective communication, area managers must also ensure that any issues or concerns are addressed in a timely and professional manner. This involves listening to clients' concerns, investigating the issue thoroughly, and providing a solution that is appropriate and satisfactory.

To manage client relations effectively, area managers must also have a strong understanding of the cleaning industry and be able to offer guidance and support to clients when necessary. This may involve providing advice on best practices for cleaning and maintenance, as well as recommending new products or services that could benefit the client.

Furthermore, area managers must have strong leadership skills and be able to manage their team effectively in order to ensure that the client's needs are met. This involves setting clear expectations, providing regular feedback and training, and addressing any performance issues in a timely and appropriate manner.

Ultimately, the success of an area manager's role in managing client relations depends on their ability to build and maintain strong, positive relationships with their clients. By being responsive, proactive, and attentive to their needs, area managers can ensure that their clients are satisfied with the services provided and that the business relationship continues to thrive.

Remember, not to over promise and under deliver.

Service Delivery - Managing Planned and Unplanned Events

Planning for Efficient Service Delivery:

To ensure efficient and high-quality service delivery as an area manager in the cleaning industry, it is necessary to develop comprehensive plans that account for both routine and unforeseen events. Area managers can optimise resources, minimise disruptions, and maintain customer satisfaction through proactive planning and effective management of scheduled and unscheduled tasks. Here is how to plan and respond to various situations:

Daily Activity Scheduling

a. Assessing Workload: Initiate by assessing the staffing and workload requirements for each site. Consider factors such as the size of the facility, the extent of the cleaning duties, client expectations, and the available workforce.

b. Establishing Cleaning Routines: Create detailed cleaning schedules that specify the tasks, frequency, and staff members responsible for each area. Consider the facility's operational hours as well as any special requirements.

c. Resource Allocation: Distribute cleaning equipment, supplies, and personnel based on the needs of each location. Ensure that the necessary resources are accessible and efficiently distributed.

d. Training and Development: Offer your cleaning staff opportunities for ongoing training and development to improve their skills, productivity, and understanding of site-specific requirements.

e. Floor Maintenance: Plan and schedule routine floor maintenance tasks such as buffing, stripping, and redressing. Determine the optimal timing with the site managers and clients to minimise disruption and ensure optimal results.

Managing Unplanned Situations

a. Establish a maintenance schedule for cleaning equipment, ensuring that it is regularly inspected, serviced, and replaced as needed. This aids in preventing breakdowns and ensures that the equipment is in optimal condition for the efficient delivery of services.

b. Emergency Response: Develop a clear emergency response plan to address unplanned situations such as floods, spills, and accidents. Assign responsibilities, establish channels of communication, and ensure that your team is trained to handle emergencies in an efficient and safe manner.

c. Prepare for potential disruptions, such as staff shortages, equipment failures, and supply shortages. Develop contingency plans to address these situations immediately, minimising the impact on service delivery and client satisfaction.

f. Communication: Maintain open lines of communication with site managers, clients, and cleaning staff in order to promptly address any unanticipated problems or emergencies. Communication must be timely and effective for problem resolution and client relationship management to be successful.

g. Deep Cleaning and Periodic Tasks: Identify periodic tasks, such as carpet cleaning, window cleaning, floor maintenance. Considering the required frequency and potential impact on daily operations, incorporate these tasks into the cleaning schedules.

By taking a proactive approach to service delivery planning, area managers can ensure day-to-day operations run smoothly and effectively manage both planned and unforeseen situations. Area managers will be able to meet client expectations, maintain high standards of cleanliness, and effectively respond to unforeseen challenges if they have a well-structured plan, efficient resource allocation, and clear communication channels.

Health and Safety

As an area manager in the cleaning industry, one of the most important aspects of your job is ensuring the health and safety of your team and anyone else who may be impacted by your work. In order to fulfil this responsibility, an area manager must understand their role and responsibilities in regard to health and safety.

First and foremost, an area manager is responsible for developing and implementing health and safety policies and procedures for their team. This includes identifying potential hazards and taking steps to mitigate or eliminate them, such as providing personal protective equipment (PPE) or modifying work processes. It is also important for the area manager to ensure that all team members are properly trained in these policies and procedures, and that they are followed consistently across all sites.

Another important responsibility of an area manager in regard to health and safety is conducting regular inspections and audits of work sites. This includes identifying any potential hazards or safety risks and taking steps to address them, as well as ensuring that all equipment and machinery is properly maintained and in good working condition.

To ensure that health and safety regulations are being followed at all times. In order to achieve this, there are several documents that an area manager may be expected to produce or manage:

1. Risk Assessments: Area managers may need to conduct regular risk assessments at each site to identify any hazards or potential risks. These assessments should be documented and reviewed on a regular basis.
2. Method Statements: Method statements outline the procedures and steps that should be taken to carry out a specific task or job safely. Area managers may be expected to create and manage these documents for all site-specific tasks.
3. Safety Audits: Safety audits are conducted to identify any potential hazards or risks that may exist on a site. Area managers may be responsible for conducting these audits or ensuring that they are carried out regularly.
4. Training Records: Area managers are responsible for ensuring that all employees receive appropriate health and safety training. This includes maintaining records of all training that has been provided.
5. Accident Reports: If an accident or incident occurs on a site, an area manager may be responsible for completing an accident report. This report should detail the cause of the incident, the steps taken to prevent it from happening again, and any corrective actions that were taken.

Additionally, an area manager should be knowledgeable about relevant health and safety legislation and regulations and should work to ensure that their team is in compliance with these requirements. This may involve working with regulatory bodies or third-party auditors to ensure that all necessary permits and licenses are in place and that all work is being done in accordance with relevant standards.

Finally, an area manager must be prepared to respond to any health and safety incidents or emergencies that may arise. This may involve investigating accidents or incidents, providing support and guidance to affected team members, and working with relevant stakeholders (such as regulators, clients, or insurance providers) to ensure that appropriate action is taken.

Overall, the role and responsibilities of an area manager in regard to health and safety are critical to the success and sustainability of any cleaning operation. By developing and implementing effective policies and procedures, conducting regular inspections and audits, staying up to date with relevant legislation and regulations, and responding promptly and effectively to incidents, an area manager can help ensure the health and safety of their team and the success of their operation.

Managing Lone Workers - Ensuring Safety and Support

Working alone on-site presents unique challenges in terms of safety and well-being for employees. As an area manager, it is essential to implement effective strategies to manage and support lone workers. By prioritising their safety, providing appropriate training, and establishing clear communication channels, you can create a secure working environment. Here's how to effectively manage lone workers:

1. Risk Assessment and Safety Measures:

1.1. Conduct a thorough risk assessment specific to lone working situations. Identify potential hazards, such as physical risks, emergency situations, or risks associated with specific tasks.

1.2. Implement necessary safety measures to mitigate risks, such as providing personal protective equipment (PPE), ensuring proper lighting, installing security systems, and establishing emergency protocols.

1.3. Regularly review and update risk assessments to address changing circumstances and new risks that may arise.

2. Lone Worker Training and Awareness:

2.1. Provide comprehensive training for lone workers, including awareness of potential risks, emergency procedures, and safe work practices. Ensure they understand the specific protocols and precautions relevant to their work environment.

2.2. Train lone workers on using safety equipment, such as personal alarms or communication devices, and ensure they know how to use them effectively.

2.3. Encourage lone workers to report any safety concerns promptly and provide guidance on incident reporting procedures.

3. Regular Check-Ins and Communication:

3.1. Establish regular check-in procedures to maintain contact with lone workers throughout their shifts. This can be done through scheduled phone calls, text messages, or using dedicated lone worker monitoring systems.

3.2. Encourage lone workers to establish regular communication with their supervisors, colleagues, or designated contacts. This enables them to report any issues or seek assistance when needed.

3.3. Establish a clear escalation procedure in case of emergencies or non-response from a lone worker. This ensures prompt action can be taken to ensure their safety.

4. Support and Well-being:

4.1. Prioritise the well-being of lone workers by providing appropriate support mechanisms. This includes regular contact with supervisors or designated colleagues to address any concerns, provide guidance, and offer emotional support.

4.2. Foster a culture of support and openness, encouraging lone workers to share their experiences, concerns, and suggestions for improving safety and well-being.

4.3. Consider implementing employee assistance programs or mental health support resources to address any psychological or emotional challenges faced by lone workers.

5. Review and Continuous Improvement:

5.1. Regularly review and evaluate the effectiveness of lone worker management strategies. Seek feedback from lone workers, supervisors, and other stakeholders to identify areas for improvement.

5.2. Stay up to date with industry best practices, regulatory requirements, and technological advancements that can enhance lone worker safety and support.

5.3. Adapt and refine the management approach based on lessons learned, changing circumstances, and feedback received.

By implementing robust safety measures, providing adequate training and support, and maintaining open lines of communication, area managers can effectively manage lone workers and ensure their safety and well-being. It is crucial to prioritise the unique needs of lone workers and continuously strive for improvement in their management and support.

Quality inspections

How should an area manager deals with quality inspections:

Quality inspections is an essential part of the role of an area manager in a cleaning company. It involves ensuring that the cleaning services provided by the company are of the highest quality and meet the expectations of the clients.

One of the key responsibilities of an area manager in quality inspections is to carry out regular inspections of the sites managed by their team. This involves conducting detailed audits of the cleaning services provided, checking that all tasks have been completed to the required standard and identifying any areas where improvements are needed.

The area manager must then work with their team to address any issues identified during the inspection process. This may involve providing additional training to the cleaning staff or implementing new processes to improve the quality of the cleaning services provided.

Another important aspect of quality inspections for an area manager is managing client feedback. They must ensure that any complaints or issues raised by clients are addressed promptly and effectively, and that steps are taken to prevent similar issues from arising in the future.

To support effective quality inspections, an area manager must also ensure that their team has the necessary equipment and resources to carry out their work to the required standard. This may involve sourcing new equipment or supplies or ensuring that existing equipment is properly maintained and serviced.

Implementing a robust quality inspections system involves various steps, including planning, measuring, analysing, and implementing corrective actions. Here are some of the methods an area manager can use to implement quality inspections:

1. **Planning:** The first step in implementing a quality control system is to develop a quality plan that outlines the company's quality goals, objectives, and expectations. The plan should also include a clear description of the cleaning processes, procedures, and standards that the company will follow.
2. **Measuring:** The next step is to measure the quality of the cleaning services provided by the company. This can be done by developing performance matrix that track the cleaning processes' effectiveness. The matrix should be designed to measure critical aspects of the cleaning process, such as the frequency of cleaning, the quality of the cleaning, and the time taken to complete the task.
3. **Analysing:** Once the data is collected, it needs to be analysed to identify areas of improvement. This involves identifying the root causes of quality issues and developing solutions to address them. The analysis

should involve input from both the area manager and the site managers responsible for the cleaning activities.

4. Corrective Actions: The final step is to implement corrective actions to address the identified quality issues. The corrective actions may include changes to the cleaning processes, additional staff training, or the introduction of new cleaning equipment. The area manager should work closely with the site managers to ensure that the corrective actions are effective and sustainable.

Implementing a quality inspections system is an ongoing process that requires continuous improvement and monitoring. The area manager must work closely with the site managers to ensure that the quality standards are maintained consistently. By implementing a robust quality inspections system, the area manager can ensure that the company provides high-quality cleaning services to its clients and maintains a competitive edge in the industry.

Business Development

As an area manager, one of your key responsibilities will be to oversee the business development activities for your region. This involves developing and implementing strategies to grow the business and increase revenue, as well as maintaining existing client relationships to ensure continued business.

One of the first steps in business development is to conduct market research and identify potential new clients. This could involve researching companies in your region that may require cleaning services, as well as identifying new trends or opportunities in the industry.

Once potential clients have been identified, it is important to build strong relationships with them. This could involve meeting with clients to discuss their needs, providing customised proposals and solutions, and ensuring that all commitments are met. As the area manager, you will need to work closely with the sales team to ensure that all business development activities are aligned with the company's overall sales strategy.

Another important aspect of business development is to identify opportunities for upselling and cross-selling. This could involve identifying additional services that could be provided to existing clients or promoting new products or services to clients who have not yet tried them.

In order to be successful in business development, an area manager will need to be highly organised, have excellent communication skills, and be able to work effectively with a range of stakeholders. They will need to be able to develop and implement strategies, analyse data and trends, and make strategic decisions to drive business growth.

Budgetary controls and management

Staff benefits and input play a vital role in the budgetary controls and management of a region manager. Here's how to effectively manage employee salaries and inputs in your area:

Budget Planning and Preparation:

- Collaborate with senior management to establish the budgetary goals and targets for your area.
- Prepare a comprehensive budget that outlines the projected revenue, expenses, and profit margins.
- Analyse historical data, market trends, and operational needs to create an accurate and realistic budget.

Expense Monitoring and Control:

- Regularly monitor and review expenses within your region to ensure they align with the approved budget.
- Identify areas of potential overspending or cost-saving opportunities.
- Implement effective cost control measures, such as negotiating vendor contracts, optimising resource allocation, or identifying areas for efficiency improvements.

Revenue Analysis and Enhancement:

- Analyse revenue streams and identify opportunities for growth and improvement.

- ❑ Monitor pricing strategies, sales performance, and customer acquisition/retention to maximise revenue generation.
- ❑ Implement marketing and promotional initiatives to attract new clients and increase sales.

Financial Reporting:

- ❑ Prepare regular financial reports, including profit and loss statements, cash flow statements, and balance sheets.
- ❑ Analyse financial data to assess the financial health and performance of your region.
- ❑ Communicate financial information to senior management, highlighting any significant variances or areas of concern.

Wage Planning and Budgeting:

- ❑ Analyse the staffing needs for your region based on workload, customer demands, and operational requirements.
- ❑ Determine the appropriate staffing levels and allocate the appropriate budget for wages.
- ❑ Consider factors such as industry standards, local market rates, and any minimum wage-related legal or contractual obligations.

Payroll Administration:

- ❑ Ensure accurate and timely administration of payroll for your region's employees.
- ❑ Work with the HR department or payroll team to process payroll, including calculating wages, deductions, and overtime, in accordance with legal requirements and company policies.
- ❑ Monitor and verify payroll records, ensuring their accuracy and promptly resolving discrepancies.

Implement a performance management system:

- ❑ Assess employee performance and connect it to benefits.
- ❑ Establish performance goals and expectations, provide consistent feedback, and conduct performance reviews to evaluate employee output, skills, and contribution.
- ❑ Identify employees with exceptional performance who may be eligible for performance-based incentives or salary increases.

Productivity and Efficiency:

- ❑ Observe the levels of staff productivity and efficiency in your area.
- ❑ Implement strategies to maximise productivity, such as training programmes, process enhancements, and workflow improvements.

- ❑ Motivate and engage employees to increase output while maintaining quality standards.

Invest in staff development and training programmes:

- ❑ To boost skills, knowledge, and performance.
- ❑ Identify areas where employees may benefit from additional training or skill development.
- ❑ Provide opportunities for career advancement and skill development, which can have a positive effect on employee retention and satisfaction.

Assess staffing levels frequently:

- ❑ To ensure that they align with operational requirements and financial objectives.
- ❑ Modify staffing levels as necessary to maintain workload equilibrium and cost-effectiveness.
- ❑ Consider alternative staffing models, such as part-time and contract employees, to manage demand fluctuations without sacrificing service quality.

Effective budgetary controls and management are necessary for achieving financial objectives, optimising resources, and preserving the financial stability of your contracts. Regular monitoring, analysis, and strategic decision-making will assist you in achieving your financial objectives and driving the success of your cleaning business.

By managing staff wages and input effectively, you can optimise your labour costs, ensure fair compensation for employees, and maintain a productive and engaged workforce. To achieve the proper balance between staffing requirements and financial goals, routine monitoring, analysis, and adjustments are necessary.

Information Technology Skills (IT)

In today's digital age, area managers in the cleaning industry can benefit from possessing a variety of Information Technology skills in order to perform their duties effectively. Here are some essential IT abilities that can assist a area manager in their role:

1. Area managers must be competent with Microsoft Word, Excel, and PowerPoint, among other software applications. These tools can be utilised for the creation of reports, data analysis, and the delivery of presentations.
2. The ability to analyse and interpret data is essential for making sound decisions. Area managers can track key performance matrix, generate reports, and identify trends or areas for improvement if they are familiar with spreadsheet software, such as Microsoft Excel or Google Sheets.
3. Area managers need to communicate and collaborate with their team, clients, and other stakeholders using communication and collaboration tools. Effective communication and collaboration are enabled by proficiency with email clients, instant messaging platforms, video conferencing tools (e.g., Microsoft Teams, Zoom), and project management software.
4. Document Management Systems: An area manager may need to access, organise, and share a variety of

files and documents. Familiarity with document management systems (e.g., Google Drive, Microsoft SharePoint) facilitates the storage, version control, and collaboration of documents.

5. Mobile Applications and Field Reporting: During site visits, numerous area managers rely on mobile applications to streamline their work. The familiarity with mobile applications for task management, reporting, and time tracking can boost productivity and efficiency.
6. Understanding cleaning management software solutions for cleaning management are intended to streamline operations, manage work schedules, monitor performance, and track inventory. Having a fundamental understanding of this software enables area managers to utilise and maximise its features.

While area managers are not expected to be IT experts, they should possess basic troubleshooting skills to address minor technical issues and assist their team members. This includes knowledge of common computer and software-related issues and the ability to seek assistance from IT departments as needed.

It is important to note that the required IT skills may vary based on the organisation, its technological infrastructure, and the area manager's responsibilities. An area manager's IT competence and effectiveness can be enhanced through ongoing education and keeping abreast of new technologies and software applicable to the cleaning industry.

Understanding Cleaning Processes and Equipment

Cleaning processes and equipment are critical components of the cleaning industry and understanding them is essential for anyone looking to become an area manager in this field. In this segment, we will discuss the different types of cleaning processes and equipment available, as well as the various safety considerations, standards, and sustainability practices that need to be taken into account when managing cleaning operations.

There are different types of cleaning processes that an area manager should be aware of. Dry cleaning, wet cleaning, and steam cleaning are some of the most common cleaning processes that are used in the cleaning industry. Dry cleaning is effective in removing dirt and dust from fabrics, while wet cleaning involves using water and detergent to clean surfaces. Steam cleaning is used for deep cleaning and is effective in removing tough stains and grime. Each cleaning process has its own advantages and disadvantages, and it is important for area managers to know when to use each one.

Area managers should be familiar with the various types of cleaning equipment available. Vacuum cleaners, floor scrubbers, and pressure washers are some examples of cleaning equipment that are commonly used in the cleaning industry. Vacuum cleaners are useful for removing dirt and debris from carpets and floors, while floor scrubbers are effective in removing dirt and stains from hard surfaces.

Pressure washers are used for outdoor cleaning and can remove dirt and grime from concrete surfaces, walls, and vehicles. Knowing the features and functionalities of each cleaning equipment is important when managing cleaning operations.

The appropriate use of cleaning products is also essential in cleaning operations. Different types of cleaning products such as detergents, disinfectants, and degreasers are available, and they are used for various cleaning purposes. Detergents are used to remove dirt and grime from surfaces, while disinfectants are used to kill bacteria and viruses. Degreasers are used for removing grease and oil from surfaces. Safety considerations such as wearing personal protective equipment (PPE) and the safe handling of cleaning chemicals should also be taken into account.

Cleaning safety is a critical aspect that cannot be ignored. It is essential to ensure that safety is maintained at all times during cleaning operations. Cleaning staff should be trained on the safe handling of cleaning equipment and chemicals, and the use of PPE. In addition, area managers should ensure that all cleaning equipment is regularly serviced and maintained to prevent accidents and injuries.

There are various cleaning standards that need to be followed in different industries and settings. For example, healthcare facilities, food preparation areas, education and care facilities have specific cleaning standards that must be met to prevent the spread of infections and contamination. Commercial buildings also have cleaning standards to ensure that the premises are clean and safe for employees and customers.

Quality assurance is an essential aspect of cleaning operations. Regular inspections, customer feedback, and employee training are some of the methods that can be used to ensure quality assurance in cleaning operations. By having an effective quality assurance program, area managers can ensure that the cleaning standards are met consistently.

Finally, sustainability in cleaning practices is becoming increasingly important. Green cleaning programs, eco-friendly cleaning products, and equipment are some of the sustainability practices that can be implemented in cleaning operations. By implementing sustainable cleaning practices, area managers can reduce the environmental impact of cleaning operations.

Managing Cleaning Staff and Operations

As an area manager in the cleaning industry, managing cleaning staff and operations is an integral part of your job. You are responsible for ensuring that cleaning operations are carried out efficiently and effectively while maintaining high levels of quality and safety.

One of the most important aspects of managing cleaning staff is recruitment and training. Area managers must ensure that the cleaning staff they hire are qualified, experienced, and reliable. This can involve conducting interviews, reference checks, and background checks to ensure that staff are trustworthy and suitable for the job. Once hired, staff must undergo thorough training to ensure that they understand the cleaning processes, equipment, and safety procedures.

Another important aspect of managing cleaning staff is scheduling and task allocation. Area managers must ensure that staff are allocated to the appropriate cleaning tasks and that the cleaning schedules are met. This can involve creating cleaning schedules, delegating tasks, and monitoring staff performance to ensure that cleaning operations are running smoothly.

Area managers must also ensure that staff are motivated, supported, and supervised. Regular feedback, coaching, and recognition of staff accomplishments can help to motivate staff and increase job satisfaction. Providing staff with the necessary resources, equipment, and support can help them to carry out their tasks efficiently and effectively.

Area managers can foster a productive and motivated workforce, resulting in high-quality cleaning services and satisfied customers.

- One effective way to manage staff in the cleaning industry is to delegate responsibilities and empower employees to take ownership of their work. By giving employees more autonomy and decision-making power, they are more likely to feel invested in their work and motivated to perform well.
- It is also important to foster a culture of open and honest communication, where employees feel comfortable sharing feedback and ideas. This includes creating opportunities for employees to provide feedback on their work environment, as well as soliciting their input on new initiatives or process improvements.
- In addition to providing ongoing training and development opportunities, it is also important to offer competitive compensation and benefits packages to attract and retain top talent. This includes ensuring that pay rates are in line with industry standards, as well as offering benefits such as health insurance and retirement plans.

- It is important to be proactive in addressing any workplace issues or conflicts that arise. This includes conducting regular performance evaluations, addressing employee concerns or grievances in a timely and respectful manner, and taking steps to create a safe and respectful work environment for all employees.

In addition to managing cleaning staff, area managers must also manage cleaning operations. This can involve overseeing the inventory of cleaning supplies, equipment, and chemicals. Ensuring that adequate supplies are available and that equipment is regularly maintained and serviced is essential for efficient cleaning operations.

Area managers must also monitor the quality of cleaning operations and ensure that cleaning standards are met consistently. Regular inspections, customer feedback, and employee training can help to ensure that cleaning operations are carried out to a high standard. Any issues or concerns must be addressed promptly to ensure that the cleaning standards are maintained.

Lastly, area managers must be able to manage cleaning operations within budget constraints. This can involve creating and managing budgets, tracking expenses, and identifying opportunities to reduce costs. Effective budget management can help to ensure that cleaning operations are carried out efficiently without compromising quality and safety.

In summary, managing cleaning staff and operations is an essential aspect of area management in the cleaning industry. Area managers must ensure that cleaning staff are recruited, trained, and supported appropriately, that cleaning operations are carried out efficiently, that cleaning standards are met consistently, and that budgets are managed effectively. Effective management of cleaning staff and operations can help to ensure that cleaning operations are carried out efficiently and effectively while maintaining high levels of quality and safety.

Training

An area manager in a cleaning company can expect to undergo a variety of training programs to carry out their role effectively. Here are some of the typical training programs an area manager may undertake:

- ❑ **Cleaning Techniques and Processes:** As an area manager, you will be responsible for ensuring that your team is delivering high-quality cleaning services to clients. Therefore, it is important to have a thorough understanding of the various cleaning techniques and processes. This may include training in areas such as chemical handling, equipment operation, and surface-specific cleaning techniques.

- ❑ **Health and Safety:** Ensuring a safe work environment is essential in the cleaning industry. Area managers should receive training on health and safety regulations, risk assessment, and hazard identification. This training should also cover the proper use of personal protective equipment (PPE) and the management of hazardous materials.
- ❑ **Management and Leadership:** An area manager must be an effective leader and manager. Training in this area may include courses on communication, motivation, team building, time management, and conflict resolution. These skills will help area managers to build strong relationships with their team, improve performance, and increase productivity.
- ❑ **Customer Service:** Area managers must have strong customer service skills to build and maintain positive relationships with clients. Training in this area may include topics such as effective communication, problem-solving, and conflict resolution.
- ❑ **Financial Management:** Area managers are often responsible for managing the financial performance of their sites. Therefore, training in financial

management may include topics such as budgeting, forecasting, cost control, and financial reporting.

- **Compliance and Regulatory Training:** Area managers must ensure that their sites comply with all relevant laws, regulations, and industry standards. Training in this area may include courses on legal compliance, environmental regulations, and quality assurance.
- **Technical Training:** In addition to general management and cleaning-related training, area managers may also need to undertake technical training to understand the specific systems, software, or equipment used by their company.

Your peers and company directors

As an area manager in the cleaning industry, it is important to have a strong working relationship with both your peers and company directors. These relationships are critical to the success of your role and your ability to effectively manage your team.

From your peers, you should expect collaboration and support. This includes working together to solve problems and sharing best practices to improve the performance of your teams. You should also expect your peers to provide feedback and constructive criticism to help you improve in your role.

From company directors, you should expect guidance and direction. This includes setting clear expectations for your role and the performance of your teams, as well as providing the necessary resources and support to help you achieve these goals. You should also expect regular communication and feedback from company directors to ensure that you are meeting their expectations and that your work aligns with the overall goals of the company.

In addition, you should expect your peers and company directors to provide a safe and supportive work environment. This includes promoting a culture of respect and collaboration, as well as providing the necessary training and resources to ensure the safety and well-being of your team members.

Finally, as an area manager, you should also hold yourself accountable for your own performance and the performance of your team. This includes regularly reviewing your own performance and seeking feedback from your peers and company directors to identify areas for improvement. By taking a proactive approach to your role and fostering strong relationships with your peers and company directors, you can effectively manage your team and achieve success in your role.

Conclusion

In conclusion, being an area manager for a cleaning company is a challenging but rewarding role. It requires a combination of technical skills, people management skills, and business acumen to effectively manage your teams and meet the needs of your clients.

Throughout this book, we have explored the key responsibilities and best practices for area managers in the cleaning industry. We have covered topics such as team management, client relations, health and safety, and financial management.

We have also discussed the importance of communication, collaboration, and continuous improvement in this role. Effective communication is critical to building strong relationships with your team members, clients, and company directors. Collaboration is key to finding solutions to complex problems and sharing best practices to improve the performance of your teams. Continuous improvement is essential to staying competitive in a constantly evolving industry and meeting the changing needs of your clients.

As an area manager, it is important to prioritise the safety and well-being of your team members, provide them with the necessary training and resources, and recognise and reward their contributions to your team's success. You should also foster a culture of respect and collaboration, where team members feel valued and supported.

In addition, it is important to stay up to date with industry trends and best practices, as well as new technologies and innovations. By staying informed and adopting new practices and technologies, you can enhance the performance of your teams, meet the changing needs of your clients, and stay ahead of the competition.

Ultimately, being an area manager for a cleaning company requires hard work, dedication, and a commitment to continuous improvement. By following the best practices and principles outlined in this book, you can effectively manage your team, meet the needs of your clients, and achieve success in this challenging but rewarding role.

Appendix 1. Sample Area Manager Job description

Job Title: Area Manager

The Area Manager is responsible for overseeing the operations of multiple cleaning sites within a designated area. The Area Manager is responsible for managing a team of supervisors and cleaning operatives to ensure the delivery of high-quality cleaning services to clients. They are also responsible for maintaining strong relationships with clients and ensuring that the business meets or exceeds its financial targets.

Key Responsibilities:

- Oversee the day-to-day operations of multiple cleaning sites within a designated area.
- Ensure that the cleaning services provided by the team meet or exceed client expectations and comply with all relevant health and safety regulations.
- Manage and motivate a team of supervisors and cleaning operatives to deliver high-quality services to clients.
- Monitor and control costs to ensure that the business meets or exceeds its financial targets.
- Develop and maintain strong relationships with clients to ensure client satisfaction and long-term partnerships.
- Provide regular reports on site performance to senior management.

- Ensure that all employees are properly trained and equipped to carry out their responsibilities.
- Conduct regular performance evaluations of supervisors and cleaning operatives to identify training needs and ensure high performance standards.
- Participate in the development and implementation of company-wide policies and procedures.

Qualifications:

- A minimum of 5 years' experience in a supervisory or management role in the cleaning industry.
- Knowledge of cleaning processes and techniques.
- Strong leadership and management skills.
- Excellent communication and interpersonal skills.
- Ability to manage multiple tasks and priorities.
- Proficient in Microsoft Office applications.
- A valid driver's license.

Salary Expectations:

The salary for an Area Manager in the cleaning industry can vary depending on the region and level of experience. In the UK, the salary range for an Area Manager is typically between £25,000 and £45,000 per annum. This may vary depending on factors such as location, company size, and level of responsibility. Additionally, some companies may offer performance-based bonuses or incentives.

Appendix 2. Types of Training to consider

1. The following training should be provided to area managers, along with the corresponding level of certification:
    - Instruction in general cleaning techniques, such as dusting, sweeping, mopping, and vacuuming.

Level of Certification: Fundamental or Foundation Cleaning Certificate.

2. Health and Safety: -
    - Training on identifying and mitigating potential workplace hazards, proper handling of cleaning chemicals, and safe equipment operation.

Certification Level: Health and Safety in Cleaning Certification.

- Infection Control and Hygiene: - Training on proper disinfection procedures, waste disposal, and maintaining a clean environment.

Certification Level: Certificate in Infection Control and Hygiene.

3. Cleaning Particular Surfaces and Locations:

- Training in the cleaning of various surfaces and areas, including carpets, hard floors, windows, and restrooms.

Certification Level: Specialist Cleaning Certification (e.g., Carpet Cleaning Certificate, Hard Floor Maintenance Certificate).

4. Handling and Maintenance of Equipment: -
    - Instruction on the safe and effective use of cleaning equipment, including proper handling, maintenance, and troubleshooting.

Certification Level: Equipment Maintenance and Handling Certificate.

5. Customer Service and Communication: -
    - Training on effective client communication, customer needs comprehension, and quality service delivery.

Certification Level: Certificate of Customer Service Excellence.

6. Time Management and Organisation:
    - Training on techniques for effective work planning, prioritisation, and time management to maximise productivity.

Level of Certification: Certificate in Time Management and Organisational Skills.

7. Environmental Consciousness and Durability:
    - Instruction in eco-friendly cleaning techniques, waste reduction, and recycling.

Environmental Awareness and Sustainability Certificate is the level of certification.

8. Specialised Instruction:
    - Additional training in specialised areas of cleaning, such as healthcare facility cleaning, food service cleaning, and post-construction cleaning.

    Certification Level: Advanced or Specialist Certificates, depending on the field.

It is essential that area managers receive ongoing training and development to improve their skills and stay abreast of industry standards. The level of certification may vary depending on the training provider and regional cleaning regulations and standards.

Index

Printed in Great Britain
by Amazon

30055072R00046